THE YOUTUBE SUCCESS FORMULA: HOW TO MONETIZE YOUR CHANNEL AND THRIVE

Book Chapters:

1. Introduction: The Power of YouTube

2. Creating Compelling Content

3. Building Your Brand on YouTube

4. Growing Your Channel's Audience

5. Search Engine Optimization for YouTube

6. Engaging with Your Viewers

7. Monetization Strategies: Ad Revenue and Sponsorships

8. Creating and Selling Merchandise

9. Crowdfunding and Patreon: Generating Fan Support

10. Collaborations and Cross-Promotions

11. Utilizing YouTube Analytics

12. Expanding Your Presence: Multiplatform Strategies

13. Sponsored Content and Brand Deals

14. Building Your Email List and Marketing Funnel

15. Scaling Your Channel: Beyond YouTube

Book Introduction:

The Youtube Success Formula: How To Monetize Your Channel And Thrive" Is A Comprehensive Guide Designed To Help Aspiring Youtubers Turn Their Passion Into A Profitable Online Business. In Today's Digital Age, Youtube Has Emerged As A Dominant Platform, Providing Opportunities For Content Creators To Reach A Massive Audience And Generate Income. However, Many Creators Struggle To Navigate The Complexities Of Monetization And Maximize Their Earning Potential.

This book serves as a roadmap for success, offering practical advice, insider tips, and proven strategies to help you monetize your YouTube channel effectively. Whether you're a beginner looking to launch your channel or an experienced creator seeking to boost your revenue streams, this book will provide you with the tools and knowledge you need to thrive in the competitive world of online content creation.

With 15 in-depth chapters, we'll cover everything from creating compelling content and building your brand to growing your audience and optimizing your channel for search engines. You'll learn how to engage with your viewers, leverage analytics to make data-driven decisions, and explore various monetization avenues such as ad revenue, sponsorships, merchandise sales, crowdfunding, and more. We'll also delve into the realm of collaborations, cross-promotions, and expanding your presence beyond YouTube to diversify your income streams.

By following the strategies outlined in this book, you'll gain a solid understanding of the YouTube ecosystem and unlock the potential to earn a sustainable income from your channel. It's time to turn your passion into profit and embark on an exciting journey toward YouTube success.

Chapter 1: Introduction to YouTube Monetization

Chapter 2: Creating Compelling Content

Chapter 3: Building Your Brand on YouTube

Chapter 4: Growing Your Channel's Audience

Chapter 5: Search Engine Optimization for YouTube

Chapter 6: Engaging with Your Viewers

Chapter 7: Monetization Strategies: Ad Revenue and Sponsorships

Chapter 8: Creating and Selling Merchandise

Chapter 9: Crowdfunding and Patreon: Generating Fan Support

Chapter 10: Collaborations and Cross-Promotions

Chapter 11: Utilizing YouTube Analytics

Chapter 12: Expanding Your Presence: Multiplatform Strategies

Chapter 13: Sponsored Content and Brand Deals

Chapter 14: Building Your Email List and Marketing Funnel

Chapter 15: Scaling Your Channel: Beyond YouTube

CHAPTER 1: INTRODUCTION TO YOUTUBE MONETIZATION

Welcome to the exciting world of YouTube monetization! In this chapter, we will lay the foundation for your journey towards turning your YouTube channel into a profitable venture. You'll gain a clear understanding of the different ways you can monetize your content and the essential steps you need to take to get started.

1.1 The Power of YouTube

YouTube has revolutionized the way we consume video content, offering a platform where creators can showcase their talent, expertise, and creativity to a global audience. With over 2 billion logged-in monthly users, YouTube presents an unparalleled opportunity to connect with people who share your passions and interests.

1.2 Monetization: Beyond Passion and Hobby

While many creators start on YouTube purely out of passion or as a hobby, it's essential to recognize the potential for financial gain. Monetizing your channel allows you to dedicate more time and resources to producing high-quality content while also earning a living from your creative endeavors.

1.3 Eligibility Requirements

Before you can begin monetizing your channel, you need to meet certain eligibility requirements set by YouTube. These include having at least 1,000 subscribers and 4,000 watch hours in the past 12 months. Once you achieve these milestones, you can apply for the YouTube Partner Program (YPP) and gain access to various monetization features.

1.4 Ad Revenue: The Basics

One of the primary ways to monetize your YouTube channel is through ad revenue. YouTube's advertising system allows creators to earn a portion of the revenue generated from ads displayed on their videos. As your channel grows and attracts more viewers, advertisers will be interested in displaying their ads alongside your content, providing you with a steady stream of income.

1.5 Sponsorships and Brand Deals

Sponsorships and brand deals are another lucrative avenue for monetization. As your channel gains popularity, brands within your niche may approach you to promote their products or services. These partnerships can be mutually beneficial, allowing you to earn money while offering valuable recommendations to your audience.

1.6 Affiliate Marketing

Affiliate marketing involves promoting products or services and earning a commission for every sale or action generated through your unique affiliate links. By partnering with relevant affiliate programs, you can recommend products you genuinely believe in and earn a commission when your viewers make a purchase.

1.7 Crowdfunding and Fan Support

Crowdfunding platforms like Patreon offer a way for your viewers to support your channel financially. By offering exclusive perks and rewards to your patrons, you can create a dedicated community that contributes to your ongoing content creation efforts.

1.8 Creating and Selling Merchandise

Merchandise sales provide an opportunity to monetize your channel while simultaneously strengthening your brand. You can design and sell branded merchandise such as t-shirts, mugs, or even digital products like e-books or online courses. These items not only generate revenue but also serve as a way for your audience to show their support and become brand advocates.

1.9 Diversifying Your Revenue Streams

To build a sustainable income from your YouTube channel, it's crucial to diversify your revenue streams. Relying solely on ad revenue leaves you vulnerable to fluctuations in advertising rates and YouTube's algorithm changes. By exploring multiple monetization avenues, you can create a more stable and resilient income model.

In this book, we will delve deeper into each of these monetization strategies, providing you with practical tips, real-life examples, and step-by-step guidance to help you navigate the complexities of YouTube monetization successfully. Get ready to unlock the true potential of your YouTube channel and embark on an exciting journey towards financial independence through your creative passions.

CHAPTER 2: CREATING COMPELLING CONTENT

In the vast sea of YouTube content, creating compelling and engaging videos is essential to attract and retain viewers. In this chapter, we will explore the key elements of crafting captivating content that resonates with your target audience. From brainstorming ideas to delivering your message effectively, you'll learn how to create videos that stand out in the crowded YouTube landscape.

2.1 Understanding Your Target Audience

Before diving into content creation, it's crucial to understand who your target audience is. What are their interests, demographics, and preferences? Conducting thorough audience research will enable you to tailor your content to their needs and desires, increasing the chances of connecting with them on a deeper level.

2.2 Brainstorming Ideas

Coming up with fresh and engaging video ideas can be a challenge, but it's a vital step in creating compelling content. Brainstorming sessions, whether individually or with a team, can spark creativity and generate a pool of potential video concepts. Consider your audience's pain points, interests, and trending topics within your niche for inspiration.

2.3 Defining Your Unique Selling Proposition (USP)

With countless YouTube channels covering similar topics, it's crucial to define your unique selling proposition (USP). What sets you apart from others? Identify your strengths, passions, and expertise that make your content unique. Your USP will attract viewers who resonate with your style and perspective.

2.4 Planning and Scripting

Effective planning and scripting play a significant role in creating engaging videos. Outline the structure of your video, including an attention-grabbing introduction, well-organized main content, and a compelling conclusion. A script or outline will help you stay focused, deliver your message clearly, and maintain a smooth flow throughout your video.

2.5 Captivating Introductions

The first few seconds of your video are crucial for capturing viewers' attention. Craft a captivating introduction that hooks your audience and entices them to watch further. Consider using intriguing questions, compelling stories, or visually striking moments to captivate viewers from the get-go.

2.6 Compelling Storytelling

Storytelling is a powerful tool for engaging your audience emotionally and keeping them invested in your content. Whether you're sharing personal experiences, case studies, or narratives related to your topic, weaving a compelling story adds depth and resonance to your videos.

2.7 Visual and Audio Quality

High-quality visuals and audio are essential for creating a professional and immersive viewing experience. Invest in a decent camera and microphone to capture clear visuals and crisp audio. Pay attention to lighting, framing, and editing techniques to enhance the visual appeal of your videos.

2.8 Engaging Delivery and Personality

Your on-screen presence and personality significantly impact viewer engagement. Be authentic, enthusiastic, and relatable while presenting your content. Establish a connection with your audience through engaging eye contact, natural gestures, and a conversational tone. Injecting your unique personality into your videos helps viewers connect with you on a personal level.

2.9 Value and Education

Providing value to your audience should be a top priority. Educate, entertain, or inspire them with every video you create. Offer actionable tips, expert insights, or thought-provoking ideas that leave a lasting impact on your viewers. Focus on solving their problems or fulfilling their desires, and they'll keep coming back for more.

2.10 Engaging Visuals and Editing Techniques

Utilize visually appealing graphics, animations, and b-roll footage to enhance the visual storytelling of your videos. Skillful editing techniques such as jump cuts, transitions, and overlays can add a professional touch and maintain the viewer's interest throughout the video.

By implementing these strategies and techniques, you'll be well on your way to creating compelling content that captivates your audience and sets your YouTube

channel apart. In the next chapter, we will delve into the crucial aspect of building your brand on YouTube, establishing a unique identity that resonates with your audience and sets you up for long-term success. Prepare to unlock the secrets of effective branding and channel growth.

CHAPTER 3: BUILDING YOUR BRAND ON YOUTUBE

Your brand is more than just a logo or a channel name; it's the identity and reputation you cultivate on YouTube. In this chapter, we will explore the key elements of building a strong brand presence that sets you apart from the competition and fosters a loyal community of viewers.

3.1 Defining Your Brand Identity

To build a successful brand, you need to have a clear understanding of your values, mission, and target audience. Define your niche, determine the tone and style of your content, and establish a consistent brand voice that aligns with your personality and resonates with your viewers.

3.2 Channel Name and Logo

Choose a channel name that reflects your brand identity and is easy to remember. Consider incorporating relevant keywords or your own name, depending on the nature of your content. Design a professional and visually appealing logo that represents your channel and can be easily recognized across different platforms.

3.3 Channel Art and Thumbnails

Eye-catching channel art and thumbnails are essential for grabbing viewers' attention and enticing them to click on your videos. Create visually appealing and cohesive graphics that convey your brand's style, message, and value proposition. Use compelling thumbnails that highlight the content and evoke curiosity.

3.4 Consistent Visual Branding

Consistency in visual branding strengthens your brand's recognition and builds trust with your audience. Establish a consistent color palette, font selection, and graphic style that aligns with your brand identity. Apply these visual elements consistently across your channel art, thumbnails, video intros, and outros.

3.5 Channel Trailer

A channel trailer is a powerful tool for introducing new viewers to your content and enticing them to subscribe. Create a short, compelling video that showcases the essence of your channel, highlights your best content, and clearly communicates the value viewers can expect by subscribing.

3.6 Branding in Video Content

Infuse your brand into your video content through intros, outros, lower thirds, and watermarks. Incorporate your logo, brand colors, and consistent graphic elements that reinforce your brand identity. Use these branding elements strategically to enhance brand recognition and create a cohesive viewing experience.

3.7 Engaging with Your Community

Building a strong brand goes beyond visual elements; it involves actively engaging with your community. Respond to comments, show appreciation for feedback, and foster a sense of belonging among your viewers. Encourage discussions, ask for input, and create opportunities for your audience to participate and feel heard.

3.8 Collaborations and Cross-Promotions

Collaborating with other YouTubers in your niche can help expand your reach and expose your brand to new audiences. Seek opportunities for collaborations and cross-promotions, where you can share audiences and create mutually beneficial content. Choose collaborators whose brand aligns with yours to maintain consistency and authenticity.

3.9 Building an Email List

An email list is a valuable asset for nurturing your relationship with your audience outside of YouTube. Offer incentives such as exclusive content, giveaways, or insider updates to encourage viewers to subscribe to your email list. Use email marketing to stay connected, share valuable content, and promote your videos and products.

3.10 Branding Beyond YouTube

Extend your brand's reach beyond YouTube by establishing a presence on other social media platforms and your own website or blog. Consistently apply your brand elements across these platforms to create a cohesive online presence. Leverage each platform's strengths to engage with your audience and attract new viewers.

By focusing on building a strong brand identity and fostering an engaged community, you'll be well on your way to creating a thriving YouTube channel. In the next chapter, we will explore the various strategies for growing your subscriber base and increasing your channel's visibility. Get ready to amplify your reach and attract a loyal following.

CHAPTER 4: GROWING YOUR YOUTUBE CHANNEL

In Chapter 3, we explored the fundamentals of building a strong brand presence on YouTube. Now, let's delve into the strategies and techniques that will help you grow your channel and reach a wider audience. From optimizing your content for search to leveraging social media, this chapter will equip you with the tools you need to accelerate your channel's growth.

4.1 Search Engine Optimization (SEO)

Optimizing your content for search engines is vital for increasing your channel's discoverability. Conduct keyword research to identify popular and relevant search terms within your niche. Incorporate these keywords strategically in your video titles, descriptions, tags, and captions to improve your ranking in search results.

4.2 Compelling Thumbnails and Titles

Thumbnails and titles are the first impressions viewers have of your videos. Create compelling and visually appealing thumbnails that accurately represent the content and pique viewers' curiosity. Pair them with attention-grabbing titles that are concise, descriptive, and incorporate relevant keywords.

4.3 Engaging Video Descriptions

Craft informative and engaging video descriptions that provide a summary of your content and entice viewers to watch. Use keywords naturally within your descriptions while providing additional value through links to related content, timestamps, and calls-to-action.

4.4 Playlists and Video Organization

Organize your videos into playlists to make it easier for viewers to navigate your content and discover related videos. Group videos based on themes, series, or topics, allowing viewers to binge-watch your content and stay engaged with your channel for longer periods.

4.5 Collaborations and Cross-Promotion

Collaborating with other YouTubers can significantly expand your reach and attract new viewers. Seek out collaboration opportunities with creators in your niche or related niches. By cross-promoting each other's channels and featuring in each other's videos, you can tap into each other's audiences and grow together.

4.6 Leveraging Social Media

Harness the power of social media platforms to promote your YouTube channel and engage with your audience. Create profiles on platforms like Instagram, Twitter, Facebook, or TikTok and share behind-the-scenes content, teasers, and highlights from your videos. Encourage your followers to subscribe to your channel and share your content with their networks.

4.7 Engaging with Your Audience

Building a loyal and engaged audience is key to channel growth. Respond to comments, ask for feedback, and encourage viewers to participate in discussions. Engage with your audience on social media, live streams, and community posts to foster a sense of community and make your viewers feel valued.

4.8 Promoting Your Channel through Email Marketing

Utilize your email list to promote your channel and build a direct connection with your audience. Send regular updates, exclusive content, and personalized recommendations to your subscribers. Encourage them to share your videos with their friends and invite them to join your community on YouTube.

4.9 Analyzing and Adjusting Your Strategy

Regularly analyze your channel's performance using YouTube Analytics and make data-driven decisions to optimize your strategy. Monitor metrics such as watch time, audience retention, and engagement to identify trends, strengths, and areas for improvement. Adjust your content, promotion strategies, and targeting based on the insights you gather.

4.10 Staying Consistent and Persistent

Consistency and persistence are key to long-term channel growth. Stick to a regular uploading schedule to keep your audience engaged and coming back for more. Continuously refine your content, branding, and promotional efforts to align with your audience's preferences and evolving trends.

With these strategies in place, you'll be well-equipped to accelerate the growth of your YouTube channel and reach a wider audience. In the next chapter, we'll explore the various monetization options available to you and how you can start earning revenue from your content.

CHAPTER 5: SEARCH ENGINE OPTIMIZATION FOR YOUTUBE

In today's competitive YouTube landscape, having great content alone is not enough. To ensure your videos reach a wider audience and attract organic views, you need to master the art of search engine optimization (SEO) specifically tailored for YouTube. In this chapter, we'll explore the strategies and techniques that will help your videos rank higher in YouTube search results and gain visibility.

5.1 Keyword Research

Keyword research is the foundation of effective YouTube SEO. Start by brainstorming relevant topics and then use keyword research tools to identify popular search terms within your niche. Look for keywords with a high search volume and moderate competition. Incorporate these keywords naturally into your video titles, descriptions, tags, and captions.

5.2 Compelling Titles

Your video title is the first thing viewers see in search results, so it needs to be compelling and engaging. Craft concise, descriptive titles that accurately represent the content of your video and include your target keyword. Make sure the title sparks curiosity and entices viewers to click on your video.

5.3 Engaging Descriptions

Your video description provides an opportunity to give viewers more information about your content and improve your video's search visibility. Write informative, keyword-rich descriptions that summarize your video and encourage viewers to watch. Include timestamps, relevant links, and calls-to-action to enhance engagement and provide additional value.

5.4 Optimized Tags

Tags help YouTube understand the content and context of your video, aiding in search rankings. Use a mix of specific and broad tags related to your video's topic. Include your target keyword as well as variations and related terms. However, avoid using irrelevant or misleading tags that may harm your channel's reputation.

5.5 Closed Captions and Transcripts

Closed captions not only make your videos more accessible but also contribute to SEO. YouTube's automatic captions are often imperfect, so consider uploading accurate captions or providing a transcript of your video. Captions help YouTube understand the content better and make it accessible to viewers who prefer to read or watch without sound.

5.6 Eye-Catching Thumbnails

Thumbnails play a crucial role in attracting viewers and increasing click-through rates. Design visually appealing and relevant thumbnails that accurately represent your video's content. Use high-resolution images, bold fonts, and contrasting colors to create eye-catching thumbnails that stand out in search results and compel viewers to click.

5.7 Viewer Engagement Signals

YouTube takes into account various engagement signals to determine the quality and relevance of your videos. Encourage viewers to like, comment, share, and subscribe to your channel. Prompt them to engage by asking questions, inviting opinions, and fostering discussions in the comments section. Higher engagement signals indicate to YouTube that your content is valuable and deserving of higher rankings.

5.8 Playlists and Series

Organize your videos into playlists and series to improve your channel's SEO. Grouping related videos together helps YouTube understand the context and relevance of your content. Create keyword-rich playlist titles and include relevant keywords in the series' titles and descriptions. Playlists also encourage viewers to watch multiple videos, increasing overall watch time.

5.9 Collaboration and Cross-Promotion

Collaborating with other YouTubers in your niche can boost your channel's visibility and attract new viewers. Seek opportunities to collaborate on videos or participate in cross-promotions. By featuring each other's channels and videos, you tap into each other's audiences and increase your exposure.

5.10 Promoting Your Videos

Promotion is crucial for increasing the visibility of your videos.

Share your videos on your website or blog, social media platforms, and relevant online communities. Encourage your audience to share your videos with their networks. Embed your videos in blog posts or articles related to your content to drive traffic to your channel.

By implementing these SEO strategies, you can improve your YouTube channel's visibility and attract a larger audience. However, it's important to remember that SEO is an ongoing process, and it requires monitoring and adjustment based on the performance of your videos. Here are a few additional tips to optimize your YouTube SEO:

5.11 Video Length and Watch Time

YouTube values videos that keep viewers engaged for longer durations. While video length should be determined by your content's needs, aim to provide value without unnecessary fluff. Monitor audience retention metrics to understand when viewers tend to drop off, and make adjustments accordingly.

5.12 Video Quality and Production Value

Investing in the quality and production value of your videos can positively impact SEO. Ensure your videos have clear visuals, good audio quality, and effective editing. High-quality videos are more likely to be recommended by YouTube and shared by viewers, leading to increased visibility.

5.13 Encourage Subscriptions and Notifications

Building a loyal subscriber base is crucial for long-term success. Encourage viewers to subscribe to your channel and turn on notifications to receive updates whenever you upload new content. Subscribers are more likely to watch, engage with, and share your videos, which can boost your search rankings.

5.14 Monitor and Respond to Analytics

Regularly review your YouTube Analytics to gain insights into your video performance. Pay attention to metrics like watch time, audience retention, click-through rate, and engagement. Identify patterns, trends, and opportunities for improvement. Use this data to refine your content strategy and optimize future videos.

5.15 Stay Updated with YouTube's Policies and Features

YouTube's algorithm and policies are subject to change. Stay informed about any updates or changes that may affect your SEO efforts. Familiarize yourself with new features and tools introduced by YouTube and explore how you can leverage them to enhance your channel's visibility and growth.

Remember, SEO is just one piece of the puzzle. Ultimately, creating high-quality, valuable content that resonates with your audience is paramount. Combine SEO best practices with compelling storytelling, authenticity, and a genuine connection with your viewers to build a successful and thriving YouTube channel.

In the next chapter, we will dive into the various strategies and techniques for engaging with your audience and fostering a strong community around your channel.

CHAPTER 6: ENGAGING WITH YOUTUBE AUDIENCE

Building a strong and engaged community around your YouTube channel is vital for long-term success. In this chapter, we will explore effective strategies and techniques for engaging with your audience, fostering a sense of community, and creating meaningful connections that keep viewers coming back for more.

6.1 Responding to Comments

Engaging with your audience starts with responding to comments on your videos. Take the time to read and reply to comments, answering questions, acknowledging feedback, and expressing appreciation for their support. By actively participating in the comment section, you demonstrate that you value your viewers' opinions and encourage further interaction.

6.2 Asking for Feedback and Suggestions

Invite your audience to share their thoughts, ideas, and suggestions. Encourage them to provide feedback on your content, ask for video topic suggestions, or seek input on future projects. By involving your audience in the content creation process, you make them feel like valued contributors and foster a sense of ownership in your channel.

6.3 Hosting Live Q&A Sessions

Live Q&A sessions allow you to directly connect with your audience in real-time. Schedule periodic live streams where you can answer questions, share insights, and engage in meaningful conversations. Encourage viewers to submit their questions in advance or during the stream, and create an interactive and inclusive experience.

6.4 Community Tab and Posts

Utilize YouTube's Community tab and posts feature to share updates, behind-the-scenes content, polls, and announcements. This allows you to communicate with your audience outside of video uploads and engage them on a more personal level. Encourage viewers to actively participate by leaving comments, voting in polls, and sharing their opinions.

6.5 Collaboration and Shoutouts

Collaborating with other creators not only expands your reach but also provides an opportunity to introduce your audience to new content and personalities. Seek collaborations with like-minded creators and feature them in your videos. Additionally, consider giving shoutouts to loyal viewers, active community members, or creators whose work you admire.

6.6 Utilizing Social Media

Extend your engagement beyond YouTube by maintaining an active presence on social media platforms. Create dedicated accounts for your channel on platforms such as Instagram, Twitter, Facebook, or TikTok. Share updates, behind-the-scenes content, sneak peeks, and engage with your audience in a more casual and interactive manner.

6.7 Conducting Giveaways and Contests

Giveaways and contests are effective ways to reward your audience and encourage engagement. Offer prizes such as merchandise, exclusive experiences, or personalized shoutouts. Encourage viewers to participate by following specific instructions, such as liking, commenting, or sharing your videos. This fosters excitement and motivates viewers to actively engage with your content.

6.8 Organizing Meetups or Events

Depending on the size and reach of your channel, consider organizing meetups or events where you can interact with your audience in person. This provides a unique opportunity to connect on a deeper level, take photos together, and have meaningful conversations. Plan and promote these events well in advance to ensure maximum attendance.

6.9 Patron and Member Exclusives

If you have a Patreon or membership program, offer exclusive content or perks to your patrons or members. This creates a sense of exclusivity and rewards their support. Exclusive content could include behind-the-scenes footage, bloopers, early access to videos, or special live streams. Make your patrons or members feel appreciated and valued.

6.10 Listening and Adapting

Lastly, always listen to your audience and adapt your content based on their preferences and feedback. Pay attention to which videos receive the most engagement and positive feedback. Analyze viewer demographics and interests through YouTube Analytics to understand your audience better. Use this information to refine your content strategy and create videos that resonate with your audience.

As you engage with your YouTube audience, remember to be genuine, authentic, and approachable. Show appreciation for their support, respond to their comments and messages, and make an effort to build personal connections. Your audience is more likely to become loyal fans and advocates if they feel a sense of belonging and connection to your channel.

Additionally, consider hosting special events or initiatives to further engage your audience:

6.11 Virtual Hangouts or Live Chats

Organize virtual hangouts or live chats where you can interact with your audience in real-time. This can be done through platforms like Zoom, Discord, or YouTube's live chat feature. It provides a more intimate setting for conversations, Q&A sessions, or even collaborative activities with your viewers.

6.12 Fan Art Showcases

Encourage your audience to create fan art inspired by your channel or content. Dedicate a video or social media post to showcase their artwork and give credit to the creators. This not only acknowledges their talent but also strengthens the bond between you and your fans.

6.13 Community Challenges

Launch community challenges where viewers can participate and share their creations or experiences related to your channel. This could include photo challenges, DIY projects, or even recreating scenes from your videos. Recognize and feature the best submissions to encourage participation and spark creativity.

6.14 Regular Live Streams

In addition to live Q&A sessions, consider hosting regular live streams where you can interact with your audience while engaging in activities such as gaming, tutorials, or discussions on specific topics. Live streams create a real-time connection and allow for direct engagement with your viewers.

6.15 Collaborative Projects with Your Audience

Involve your audience in collaborative projects to foster a sense of community and shared creativity. This could involve creating a compilation video featuring viewer-submitted content, organizing a charity initiative together, or even co-creating content by inviting viewers to contribute ideas or segments for your videos.

Remember that engaging with your audience goes beyond just creating content—it's about building relationships, listening to feedback, and nurturing a community of supporters. Take the time to understand your audience's needs, preferences, and aspirations, and tailor your engagement strategies accordingly.

In the next chapter, we will explore various methods and strategies to monetize your YouTube channel and turn your passion into a sustainable income stream.

CHAPTER 7: MONETIZING YOUR YOUTUBE CHANNEL

Congratulations on building a successful YouTube channel! Now, let's explore different methods and strategies to monetize your content and turn your passion into a sustainable income stream.

7.1 Ad Revenue

One of the primary ways to monetize your YouTube channel is through ad revenue. YouTube's Partner Program allows eligible creators to monetize their videos by displaying ads. As your channel grows and meets the program's requirements, you can apply to join and start earning from ads that are displayed before, during, or after your videos. Remember to create engaging content that attracts advertisers and keeps viewers watching.

7.2 Sponsorships and Brand Deals

Collaborating with brands and securing sponsorships is another lucrative avenue for monetization. As your channel gains visibility and influence, brands may approach you with partnership opportunities. Alternatively, you can reach out to relevant brands that align with your content and propose collaboration ideas. Negotiate fair compensation for promoting their products or services in your videos, ensuring a seamless integration that adds value to your audience.

7.3 Merchandise and E-commerce

Leverage your channel's branding and audience loyalty to sell merchandise and other products. Design and sell branded merchandise such as t-shirts, hoodies, or accessories through platforms like Teespring, Spreadshirt, or your own e-commerce website. Additionally, consider creating digital products like e-books, online courses, or presets that cater to your audience's interests and offer them for sale.

7.4 Channel Memberships and Subscriptions

YouTube offers a channel membership feature that allows your most dedicated fans to become paid members of your channel. Memberships can provide exclusive perks like badges, custom emojis, early access to videos, or members-only live streams. Additionally, you can explore platforms like Patreon or Ko-fi to offer exclusive content, behind-the-scenes access, and personalized rewards to your loyal supporters.

7.5 Crowdfunding and Donations

If your audience is particularly supportive and wants to contribute to your channel's growth, consider setting up a crowdfunding campaign or enabling donations through platforms like PayPal or Buy Me a Coffee. This allows viewers to voluntarily contribute funds to support your content creation efforts. Offer incentives such as shoutouts, personalized messages, or exclusive content to show your appreciation.

7.6 Sponsored Content and Product Placement

Apart from traditional sponsorships, you can incorporate sponsored content and product placements in your videos. Work with brands to feature their products or services naturally within your content. Be transparent with your audience about sponsored content and maintain authenticity by only promoting products you genuinely endorse. Building trust is crucial to maintaining a loyal and engaged audience.

7.7 Licensing and Content Syndication

If you have exceptional content, consider licensing it to other platforms, media outlets, or content aggregators. This allows your videos to reach a broader audience while generating additional income. Explore opportunities to syndicate your content to television networks, online publications, or streaming services that may be interested in showcasing your work.

7.8 Public Speaking and Workshops

Leverage your expertise and credibility as a YouTube creator to secure speaking engagements or workshops. Share your knowledge, insights, and experiences at conferences, industry events, or educational institutions. Additionally, you can offer paid workshops or consultations where you provide personalized guidance and training to aspiring creators or individuals interested in your niche.

7.9 Affiliate Marketing

Affiliate marketing involves promoting products or services and earning a commission for each sale or referral made through your unique affiliate links. Research and identify affiliate programs that align with your content and recommend products or services that genuinely benefit your audience. Be transparent about your affiliate partnerships to maintain trust with your viewers.

7.10 Events, Meetups, and Fan Experiences

Consider organizing live events, meetups, or fan experiences for your audience. This could include hosting live Q&A sessions, fan meetups, workshops, or even exclusive events where fans can interact with you and fellow community members. Charge admission fees or offer premium packages that provide additional perks and experiences. These events not only generate revenue but also create memorable experiences for your dedicated audience.

7.11 YouTube Premium Revenue

YouTube Premium is a subscription-based service that offers ad-free viewing, offline playback, and access to YouTube Originals. As a YouTube Partner, you can earn a share of the revenue generated from YouTube Premium subscribers who watch your content. This additional revenue stream can contribute to your overall monetization strategy.

7.12 Sponsored Videos and Product Reviews

Similar to sponsorships, you can collaborate with brands to create dedicated sponsored videos or product reviews. In these videos, you provide an in-depth analysis, demonstration, or review of the product or service. Be transparent with your audience about the sponsored nature of the content, and focus on delivering valuable and honest insights that help your viewers make informed decisions.

7.13 Consulting and Coaching Services

If you have expertise in your niche, consider offering consulting or coaching services to individuals or businesses. This can include personalized guidance on YouTube strategies, content creation, audience engagement, or channel growth. Package your knowledge and experience into valuable services that can be delivered through one-on-one sessions, group workshops, or online courses.

7.14 Sponsored Events or Collaborative Projects

Collaborate with brands or organizations to create sponsored events or collaborative projects that align with your channel's content. This could involve hosting a live event, organizing a charity campaign, or participating in a brand's marketing initiative. These partnerships not only provide financial compensation but also expand your reach and introduce your channel to new audiences.

7.15 Licensing Music and Content

If you create original music or produce unique content, explore opportunities to license your work. Music licensing platforms like Epidemic Sound or Artlist offer a marketplace where creators can monetize their music by providing licenses to other creators, filmmakers, or businesses. Similarly, consider licensing your video content for use in commercials, documentaries, or other media productions.

Remember that monetizing your YouTube channel requires a strategic approach and a balance between revenue generation and maintaining the trust and loyalty of your audience. Be transparent, authentic, and focused on delivering value to your viewers. Continuously analyze and adapt your monetization strategies to align with your audience's interests and needs.

In the next chapter, we will discuss effective strategies for optimizing your YouTube channel's performance, increasing your subscriber count, and maximizing your overall reach and visibility.

CHAPTER 8: CREATING AND SELLING MERCHANDISE

Merchandise is a fantastic way to engage with your audience, promote your brand, and generate additional revenue. In this chapter, we will explore the process of creating and selling merchandise that resonates with your viewers and helps build a strong connection with your fanbase.

8.1 Understanding Your Audience

Before diving into merchandise creation, it's crucial to understand your audience's preferences, interests, and demographics. Analyze your viewership data, engage with your community, and gather insights through surveys or polls to gain a deep understanding of what merchandise would appeal to them the most.

8.2 Developing Your Brand Identity

A strong brand identity is essential when creating merchandise. Define your brand's values, personality, and aesthetics. Ensure that your merchandise aligns with your channel's content and resonates with your audience. Consistency in branding will help create a cohesive and recognizable image that strengthens the connection between your channel and the merchandise.

8.3 Merchandise Ideas and Designs

Brainstorm unique and creative merchandise ideas that reflect your channel's theme and resonate with your audience. Consider items such as t-shirts, hoodies, hats, mugs, phone cases, stickers, or even custom-designed collectibles. Collaborate with artists or designers to create appealing and high-quality designs that embody your brand and appeal to your viewers.

8.4 Production and Sourcing

Once you have finalized your merchandise designs, explore different production and sourcing options. You can choose to work with print-on-demand services, which handle production, shipping, and inventory management for you. Alternatively, you can opt for bulk production, where you order merchandise in larger quantities to have more control over the production process and potentially reduce costs.

8.5 Setting Pricing and Profit Margins

Determining the right pricing for your merchandise requires careful consideration. Take into account production costs, shipping expenses, and any additional fees associated with the chosen production method. Factor in a reasonable profit margin that allows you to cover your expenses while ensuring the merchandise remains affordable and attractive to your audience.

8.6 Creating an Online Store

Set up an online store to showcase and sell your merchandise. Platforms like Shopify, BigCommerce, or Etsy provide user-friendly interfaces and tools to help you create a professional-looking store. Customize your store's design to align with your brand and make it easy for your viewers to navigate, browse products, and make purchases.

8.7 Promoting Your Merchandise

Promotion is key to driving sales of your merchandise. Leverage your existing YouTube channel, social media platforms, and website to showcase your merchandise to your audience. Create engaging content around your merchandise, such as lookbook videos, unboxing videos, or testimonials. Offer exclusive discounts or limited-time offers to incentivize purchases.

8.8 Collaborations and Limited Edition Releases

Collaborating with other creators or brands can expand your reach and create unique merchandise opportunities. Consider partnering with like-minded creators for joint merchandise releases or limited edition collaborations. This not only introduces your merchandise to new audiences but also adds excitement and collectibility for your existing fans.

8.9 Fulfillment and Customer Service

Ensure smooth and efficient fulfillment of merchandise orders. Communicate clearly with your customers regarding shipping times, tracking information, and any potential delays. Provide excellent customer service by promptly addressing inquiries, concerns, or issues. Building a reputation for reliable fulfillment and exceptional customer support will enhance your brand's trustworthiness.

8.10 Tracking Sales and Adjusting Strategies

Regularly track and analyze your merchandise sales to gain insights into which items perform best and resonate with your audience. Use this data to refine your merchandise offerings, optimize designs, or introduce new products based on customer demand. Stay adaptable and open to evolving your merchandise strategy as you continue to learn from your audience's preferences.

By understanding your audience, developing a strong brand identity, creating appealing designs, and implementing effective marketing strategies, you can successfully create and sell merchandise that not only generates revenue but also strengthens your connection with your fanbase.

CHAPTER 9: CROWDFUNDING AND PATREON: GENERATING FAN SUPPORT

In this chapter, we will delve into the world of crowdfunding and Patreon, two powerful platforms that enable creators to receive direct support from their fans. These platforms provide a way for your audience to contribute financially to your channel, allowing you to further invest in your content, engage with your community, and pursue your creative endeavors.

9.1 Understanding Crowdfunding

Crowdfunding has revolutionized the way creators fund their projects and connect with their audience. Platforms such as Kickstarter, Indiegogo, and GoFundMe enable creators to set funding goals and invite their fans to contribute. You can create a compelling campaign that highlights your upcoming projects, explains how the funds will be utilized, and offers enticing rewards to those who support your campaign.

9.2 Creating a Patreon Page

Patreon is a membership-based platform that allows fans to become patrons of your work. By setting up a Patreon page, you can offer exclusive content, rewards, and experiences to your patrons in exchange for their ongoing support. These perks can include early access to videos, behind-the-scenes content, personalized messages, exclusive merchandise, or even participation in live streams or Q&A sessions.

9.3 Developing Reward Tiers

When setting up your Patreon page, it's important to create enticing reward tiers that cater to different levels of support. Design tiers that offer increasing benefits as the support level rises, providing incentives for your fans to contribute at higher levels. For example, you can offer different tiers with varying access to exclusive content, merchandise discounts, or even opportunities for one-on-one interactions.

9.4 Exclusive Content for Supporters

To incentivize fan support, create exclusive content that is available only to your patrons or crowdfunding backers. This can be in the form of bonus videos, tutorials, exclusive vlogs, or special access to events. Make your supporters feel valued and appreciated by providing them with content that goes above and beyond what is available to the general public.

9.5 Engaging with Supporters

One of the key benefits of crowdfunding and Patreon is the opportunity to build a closer relationship with your most dedicated fans. Engage with your supporters by responding to their comments, messages, and suggestions. Host live Q&A sessions or private community forums where you can interact directly with your patrons. Make them feel like a part of an exclusive community that supports and believes in your work.

9.6 Communicating Progress and Milestones

Regularly update your crowdfunding backers or Patreon supporters on the progress of your projects and milestones achieved. Transparency and open communication build trust and keep your supporters excited about the content they are helping to create. Share updates, sneak peeks, and behind-the-scenes insights to make them feel involved in your creative journey.

9.7 Collaborative Decision-Making

Involving your fans in the decision-making process can foster a sense of ownership and strengthen their connection to your channel. Seek their input on upcoming projects, video topics, or merchandise designs through polls, surveys, or exclusive discussions. This collaborative approach not only empowers your supporters but also ensures that you are creating content that resonates with your audience.

9.8 Expressing Gratitude

Always express your gratitude and appreciation to your crowdfunding backers and Patreon supporters. Acknowledge their contributions in your videos, social media posts, or on your website. Consider sending personalized thank-you notes, signed merchandise, or even hosting special events or meetups exclusively for your supporters as a gesture of gratitude for their ongoing support.

9.9 Managing Expectations

While crowdfunding and Patreon can provide significant support, it's essential to manage expectations and be transparent about the limitations of your resources and commitments. Set realistic goals, deliver on promised rewards and perks, and communicate any potential delays or changes in plans. By being honest and managing expectations, you can maintain the trust and loyalty of your supporters.

9.10 Offering Limited-time Campaigns

To keep your crowdfunding efforts fresh and engaging, consider running limited-time campaigns or special events. These can include crowdfunding drives for specific projects, milestone celebrations, or time-limited offers for exclusive merchandise or experiences. By creating a sense of urgency and exclusivity, you can incentivize your audience to participate and contribute during these special occasions.

9.11 Regularly Evaluating and Improving

Continuously assess the effectiveness of your crowdfunding and Patreon strategies. Monitor your campaign performance, analyze supporter feedback, and make adjustments as needed. Experiment with different rewards, engagement strategies, and communication methods to find what resonates most with your audience. By evolving and improving your approach, you can maximize the potential of crowdfunding and Patreon as sustainable revenue streams.

9.12 Collaboration with Other Creators

Consider collaborating with other creators on joint crowdfunding campaigns or Patreon cross-promotions. This can expand your reach, introduce you to new audiences, and create mutually beneficial partnerships. Explore opportunities to team up with creators whose content aligns with yours and whose audience may have an interest in supporting your work.

9.13 Giving Back and Supporting Causes

Use your platform and the support you receive from crowdfunding or Patreon to give back to your community or support meaningful causes. Dedicate a portion of the funds raised to support charitable organizations or initiatives that align with your values and resonate with your audience. By showcasing your commitment to making a positive impact, you can deepen the connection with your supporters.

9.14 Nurturing Long-term Relationships

Building a strong community around your crowdfunding or Patreon efforts requires nurturing long-term relationships. Regularly engage with your supporters, provide them with valuable content and experiences, and make them feel like valued members of your community. Foster a sense of belonging and appreciation, as this will encourage ongoing support and foster a sustainable fanbase.

9.15 Exploring Additional Revenue Streams

While crowdfunding and Patreon can be significant sources of fan support, it's essential to diversify your revenue streams. Explore other monetization avenues such as brand partnerships, sponsored content, merchandise sales, or even creating and selling your own digital products. By diversifying your income, you can reduce reliance on a single source and create a more stable financial foundation.

CHAPTER 10: COLLABORATIONS AND CROSS-PROMOTIONS

Collaborations and cross-promotions with other creators can be incredibly beneficial for growing your YouTube channel. By teaming up with like-minded creators, you can expand your reach, tap into new audiences, and create exciting content that captivates your viewers. In this chapter, we will explore the power of collaborations and cross-promotions and provide guidance on how to maximize their impact.

10.1 Finding Compatible Creators

When seeking collaborators, look for creators whose content aligns with your own and whose audience shares similar interests. Research popular channels within your niche and identify creators whose style, values, and target demographic complement your own. Engaging with creators who have a genuine interest in collaborating will increase the likelihood of a successful partnership.

10.2 Establishing Common Goals

Before diving into a collaboration, establish common goals and objectives with your potential partners. Discuss what you hope to achieve through the collaboration, whether it's reaching a specific milestone, expanding your subscriber base, or creating engaging content together. Aligning your goals ensures that everyone is on the same page and working towards a shared vision.

10.3 Crafting Collaborative Ideas

Brainstorm creative ideas for your collaboration that will excite both you and your partner's audience. Consider unique video concepts, challenges, or series that leverage both of your strengths and offer something fresh and compelling. Strive for a balance that showcases each creator's individuality while fostering a synergistic dynamic that captivates viewers.

10.4 Outlining Responsibilities

Once you have settled on a collaborative idea, outline the responsibilities and tasks of each creator involved. Clearly define who will handle pre-production, filming, editing, and promotion. Establishing roles and expectations upfront ensures smooth coordination and allows each creator to contribute their expertise to the collaboration's success.

10.5 Coordinating Schedules

Collaborations require careful schedule coordination. Take into account each creator's availability, time zones, and commitments to ensure a smooth production process. Plan well in advance and establish a timeline that accommodates everyone's needs. Open communication and flexibility are crucial when navigating schedules and ensuring a successful collaboration.

10.6 Promoting the Collaboration

To maximize the impact of your collaboration, develop a comprehensive promotion strategy. Coordinate with your partner to cross-promote the collaboration on both of your channels and social media platforms. Tease the collaboration to your audiences in advance to generate anticipation and excitement. Leverage the power of community tabs, social media posts, and collaboration announcement videos to amplify the reach of the collaboration.

10.7 Leveraging Each Other's Strengths

During the collaboration, capitalize on each other's strengths and unique abilities. Whether it's your partner's editing skills, storytelling prowess, or on-camera charisma, combine your talents to create content that exceeds the expectations of your viewers. Embrace the opportunity to learn from each other and elevate the quality of the collaboration.

10.8 Engaging with Combined Audiences

When collaborating with another creator, you have the opportunity to introduce your content to a whole new audience. Engage with the comments, messages, and feedback from both your audience and your collaborator's audience. Foster a welcoming and inclusive environment, and encourage viewers to explore both channels for further content.

10.9 Analyzing Collaboration Performance

After the collaboration, analyze its performance by assessing metrics such as views, engagement, subscriber growth, and audience retention. Evaluate the impact on your channel and the long-term benefits of the collaboration. Take note of the strategies and elements that resonated most with your audience and apply those learnings to future collaborations.

10.10 Building Lasting Relationships

A successful collaboration can pave the way for lasting relationships with fellow creators. Foster genuine connections by supporting each other's content, collaborating on future projects, and maintaining open communication to build a network of trusted collaborators. Stay engaged with your collaborators by regularly interacting with their content, providing feedback, and exploring opportunities for future collaborations. Building lasting relationships with creators not only expands your network but also opens doors to new collaborations and growth opportunities.

10.11 Exploring Cross-Promotion Opportunities

Beyond collaborations, consider cross-promotion opportunities with other creators. This involves featuring each other's channels or content in your videos, sharing shoutouts on social media, or participating in joint promotional campaigns. Cross-promotion allows you to tap into each other's audiences and introduce your content to a wider viewership, fostering mutual growth and engagement.

10.12 Nurturing Mutual Growth

When engaging in collaborations or cross-promotions, prioritize the mutual growth and success of all parties involved. Support your collaborators by actively promoting their content, engaging with their audience, and providing opportunities for them to shine. By nurturing mutual growth, you cultivate a supportive community of creators who uplift each other and contribute to collective success.

10.13 Embracing Diversity and Uniqueness

When seeking collaborators, embrace diversity and uniqueness.

Collaborating with creators from different backgrounds, perspectives, and styles can bring fresh perspectives and expand the horizons of your content. Celebrate the diversity within the creator community and use collaborations as a platform to share diverse voices, experiences, and stories.

10.14 Learning from Each Collaboration

Every collaboration presents an opportunity for growth and learning. Reflect on each collaboration to identify areas for improvement, refine your creative process, and enhance your collaborative skills. Take note of the aspects that worked well and those that could be enhanced, and apply these insights to future collaborations to continuously elevate your content.

10.15 Staying Authentic and True to Your Audience

While collaborations and cross-promotions can be exciting, it's crucial to stay authentic and true to your audience. Ensure that any collaborations align with your brand values, content style, and audience preferences. Maintaining consistency and authenticity in your collaborations helps build trust with your viewers and reinforces your channel's unique identity.

As we conclude this chapter, remember that collaborations and cross-promotions offer immense potential for channel growth, audience expansion, and creative exploration. Embrace the opportunity to connect with fellow creators, create captivating content together, and foster a community that thrives on collaboration.

CHAPTER 11: UTILIZING YOUTUBE ANALYTICS

YouTube Analytics is a powerful tool that provides valuable insights into your channel's performance, audience demographics, and viewer behavior. By leveraging the data and metrics available through YouTube Analytics, you can make informed decisions, optimize your content strategy, and effectively grow your channel. In this chapter, we will explore the various features and metrics of YouTube Analytics and discuss how to effectively utilize them.

11.1 Understanding YouTube Analytics

YouTube Analytics provides comprehensive data and metrics that offer deep insights into your channel's performance. It allows you to track key metrics such as views, watch time, engagement, subscriber growth, and audience demographics. By understanding and interpreting these metrics, you can gain a clear picture of your channel's strengths, areas for improvement, and audience preferences.

11.2 Analyzing Channel Performance

Start by analyzing your channel's overall performance metrics in YouTube Analytics. Examine metrics such as total views, watch time, and subscriber growth over time. Identify trends, spikes, or dips in performance and correlate them with specific videos, topics, or promotional efforts. This analysis will help you understand what resonates with your audience and inform your content strategy moving forward.

11.3 Evaluating Video Performance

YouTube Analytics provides detailed metrics for individual videos, including views, watch time, average view duration, likes, dislikes, and audience retention. Dive into the performance of your top-performing videos as well as those that may underperform. Identify patterns in successful videos, such as common themes, formats, or video lengths, and replicate those elements in future content.

11.4 Identifying Audience Demographics

Understanding your audience demographics is vital for tailoring your content to their preferences. YouTube Analytics provides insights into the age, gender, location, and interests of your viewers. Analyze this data to identify your primary audience segments and adjust your content strategy accordingly. For example, if you discover that a significant portion of your viewers are located in a particular country, consider creating content that caters to their interests or customs.

11.5 Tracking Audience Engagement

Engagement metrics, such as likes, comments, shares, and subscriber growth, offer valuable insights into how your audience interacts with your content. Analyze the engagement patterns across your videos to identify the types of content that elicit the most engagement. Encourage viewer interaction by asking questions, inviting comments, and responding to audience feedback to foster a sense of community and loyalty.

11.6 Utilizing Traffic Sources

YouTube Analytics provides information on the sources that drive traffic to your videos, including search results, suggested videos, external websites, and social media platforms. Analyze this data to understand where your viewers are discovering your content. Optimize your video titles, descriptions, and tags to improve search visibility and consider strategic collaborations or cross-promotions with creators who drive significant traffic.

11.7 Monitoring Audience Retention

Audience retention metrics reveal how long viewers watch your videos before leaving. Analyze the audience retention graph in YouTube Analytics to identify specific moments where viewers drop off. This data can help you identify areas in your videos that may need improvement, such as pacing, content delivery, or editing. Aim to create compelling content that captivates viewers and keeps them engaged throughout the video.

11.8 Testing and Iterating

YouTube Analytics empowers you to test and iterate your content strategy based on data-driven insights. Use A/B testing to experiment with different video formats, titles, thumbnails, or content styles. Monitor the performance metrics of each variant and make data-backed decisions on what works best for your audience. Continuously refine and optimize your content based on the feedback provided by YouTube Analytics.

11.9 Setting Goals and Key Performance Indicators (KPIs)

Establish clear goals and key performance indicators (KPIs) based on the metrics available in YouTube Analytics to track your channel's progress and success. Set specific, measurable goals such as increasing views, watch time, or subscriber count within a specified time frame. Use YouTube Analytics to monitor your progress towards these goals and make adjustments to your content strategy as needed.

11.10 Utilizing YouTube Studio Insights

YouTube Studio offers additional insights and analytics to further enhance your understanding of your channel's performance. Utilize features like the Reach Viewers and Audience tab to gain insights into the reach and engagement of your videos across different devices, demographics, and traffic sources. These insights can help you tailor your content and promotional efforts to effectively target specific audience segments.

11.11 Tracking Revenue and Monetization Metrics

For channels that have monetization enabled, YouTube Analytics provides metrics related to revenue, ad performance, and monetization sources. Analyze your revenue metrics to understand the impact of monetization strategies and identify opportunities for growth. Track ad performance metrics such as ad impressions, click-through rates, and revenue per thousand views (RPM) to optimize your ad placement and maximize revenue potential.

11.12 Staying Updated with YouTube Analytics

YouTube regularly updates and enhances its Analytics features. Stay informed about new features, changes, and updates to make the most of the data available to you. YouTube's Creator Academy and Help Center provide resources and tutorials to help you navigate YouTube Analytics effectively and stay up to date with the latest developments.

11.13 Integrating Analytics into Your Content Strategy

Integrate the insights gained from YouTube Analytics into your content strategy. Use the data to inform decisions on video topics, formats, duration, and audience targeting. Tailor your content to align with the preferences and interests of your audience while staying true to your unique style and voice. Regularly evaluate the impact of content adjustments based on the performance metrics provided by YouTube Analytics.

11.14 Experimenting and Innovating

YouTube Analytics should not only be used for analysis but also as a source of inspiration for experimentation and innovation. Take risks, try new formats, and explore emerging trends to keep your content fresh and engaging. Use the feedback from YouTube Analytics to iterate and improve, always striving to deliver the best possible experience to your audience.

11.15 Embracing a Data-Driven Mindset

Ultimately, embracing a data-driven mindset is crucial for leveraging YouTube Analytics effectively. Continuously monitor and analyze the data, adapt your strategies based on the insights gained, and use the feedback loop of data and experimentation to drive channel growth. By leveraging the power of YouTube Analytics, you can make informed decisions that optimize your content, engage your audience, and propel your channel towards success.

As we conclude this chapter, remember that YouTube Analytics is a valuable tool that empowers you to understand your audience, measure your channel's performance, and make data-driven decisions.

CHAPTER 12: EXPANDING YOUR PRESENCE: MULTIPLATFORM STRATEGIES

In today's digital landscape, having a strong presence on multiple platforms is essential for reaching and engaging a broader audience. By implementing multiplatform strategies, you can extend your content's reach beyond YouTube and create a cohesive brand identity across various online platforms. In this chapter, we will explore effective methods to expand your presence through multiplatform strategies.

12.1 Assessing Platform Compatibility

Before expanding your presence to other platforms, it's crucial to assess the compatibility of each platform with your content and target audience. Research popular platforms such as Instagram, Twitter, Facebook, TikTok, and Snapchat to understand their unique features, user demographics, and content formats. Choose platforms that align with your brand and offer opportunities to showcase your content effectively.

12.2 Tailoring Content for Each Platform

Each platform has its own content formats, audience expectations, and engagement dynamics. To maximize your presence, tailor your content for each platform while maintaining your brand's identity. For example, on Instagram, focus on visual storytelling through compelling images and videos, while on Twitter, engage in real-time conversations and share bite-sized updates or thoughts.

12.3 Repurposing Content

Repurposing content allows you to adapt your existing YouTube content for other platforms. Identify key moments, highlights, or valuable insights from your videos that can be transformed into standalone content pieces. For instance, you can create short video clips, quote graphics, or teaser trailers to share on platforms like Instagram, Twitter, or TikTok, driving traffic back to your YouTube channel.

12.4 Cross-Promotion Across Platforms

Leverage your presence on one platform to promote and drive traffic to your other platforms. Cross-promotion enables you to tap into existing audiences and expand your reach. Promote your YouTube channel on platforms like Instagram, Twitter, or Facebook by sharing snippets, behind-the-scenes content, or exclusive updates. Encourage your audience to follow you across platforms for a more holistic experience.

12.5 Engaging with the Community

Building a strong community is vital across all platforms.

Respond to comments, direct messages, and mentions to foster meaningful connections and show appreciation for your audience's support. Encourage discussions, ask questions, and host interactive events like live Q&A sessions or challenges to drive engagement and create a sense of belonging within your community.

12.6 Leveraging Platform-Specific Features

Each platform offers unique features and tools that can enhance your content and engagement. Explore and leverage these features to stand out and captivate your audience. For example, on TikTok, leverage trending hashtags and participate in challenges, while on Facebook, consider using live streaming or groups to connect with your audience in real-time or foster a dedicated community.

12.7 Collaborating with Influencers and Creators

Collaborating with influencers and creators from other platforms can expose your content to new audiences and broaden your reach. Identify creators whose audience aligns with your target demographic and explore opportunities for cross-platform collaborations. This could include guest appearances, joint projects, or shoutouts, benefiting both parties by expanding their respective audiences.

12.8 Analyzing Platform Performance

Track and analyze the performance of your content on each platform using their respective analytics tools. Gain insights into engagement rates, follower growth, reach, and demographics. Assess which platforms are driving the most traffic, engagement, and conversions to refine your multiplatform strategy and allocate resources accordingly.

12.9 Consistency and Branding

Maintain consistency in your branding across all platforms to create a cohesive identity. Use consistent profile images, channel banners, and brand colors to establish a recognizable presence. Align your content themes, style, and tone with your brand's values and personality to build trust and loyalty among your audience, regardless of the platform they engage with.

12.10 Managing Time and Resources

Expanding your presence to multiple platforms requires effective time and resource management. Consider the following strategies:

12.10.1 Prioritize Platforms: Identify the platforms that yield the highest engagement and align with your goals. Focus your efforts on those platforms to ensure a consistent and quality presence.

12.10.2 Batch Content Creation: Plan and create content in batches to optimize your time and ensure a steady stream of content across platforms. This approach allows you to repurpose and adapt content efficiently.

12.10.3 Automation and Scheduling: Utilize automation tools and scheduling platforms to streamline your multiplatform strategy. Schedule posts in advance, automate cross-platform sharing, and leverage analytics tools to monitor performance.

12.10.4 Delegate and Outsource: If resources allow, consider delegating tasks or outsourcing certain aspects of your multiplatform strategy. This could include social media management, content creation, or graphic design to ensure consistent quality across platforms.

12.11 Monitoring and Adjusting

Continuously monitor the performance of your multiplatform strategy and adjust accordingly. Regularly review analytics and engagement metrics to identify what resonates with your audience on each platform. Adapt your content, posting schedule, or platform selection based on the data-driven insights you gather.

12.12 Staying Updated and Experimenting

Stay informed about platform updates, trends, and emerging platforms in the digital landscape. Embrace experimentation and try new features or content formats to keep your multiplatform strategy fresh and engaging. Be willing to adapt and evolve as new opportunities arise.

12.13 Collaborating with Platform-Specific Creators

Explore collaborations with creators who specialize in specific platforms. Partnering with creators who have established audiences on platforms like Instagram, TikTok, or Twitter can provide valuable exposure and introduce your content to new viewers. Seek out opportunities for joint projects, guest appearances, or cross-promotions to leverage their platform expertise.

12.14 Building Relationships with Platform Communities

Engage authentically with communities on each platform to build relationships and establish your presence. Participate in discussions, contribute value, and support fellow creators. By fostering genuine connections, you can attract dedicated followers who will support and advocate for your content.

12.15 Embracing Growth and Adaptation

Expanding your presence to multiple platforms is an ongoing process of growth and adaptation. Continuously learn, iterate, and optimize your multiplatform strategy based on audience feedback and platform trends. Embrace the evolving nature of digital media and seize opportunities to expand your reach and impact.

As we conclude this chapter on expanding your presence through multiplatform strategies, remember that each platform offers unique opportunities to connect with audiences and expand your brand's influence. In the next chapter, we will discuss the sponsored content and brand deals.

CHAPTER 13: SPONSORED CONTENT AND BRAND DEALS

In the world of content creation, sponsored content and brand deals play a significant role in monetizing your YouTube channel and establishing partnerships with brands. This chapter will guide you through the process of creating successful sponsored content and securing brand deals that align with your channel's values and audience.

13.1 Understanding Sponsored Content

Sponsored content refers to collaborations with brands where you create content that promotes their products or services. It's important to approach sponsored content authentically and transparently, ensuring that it aligns with your channel's niche and resonates with your audience. Maintaining trust and credibility should be the foundation of any sponsored collaboration.

13.2 Identifying Relevant Brands

When seeking brand deals, focus on identifying brands that align with your content and target audience. Consider the values, interests, and needs of your viewers and research brands that cater to those demographics. Look for brands that share your channel's mission and can provide genuine value to your audience.

13.3 Building Your Brand and Audience

Brands are more likely to partner with creators who have a strong brand presence and engaged audience. Prioritize building your brand by consistently delivering high-quality content, engaging with your audience, and growing your subscriber base. Demonstrating your influence and ability to drive results will make you an attractive partner for brands.

13.4 Creating a Media Kit

A media kit is a valuable tool for showcasing your channel's statistics, audience demographics, and previous brand collaborations. Create a professional and visually appealing media kit that highlights your unique selling points and showcases your content's reach and engagement. Include relevant metrics such as views, subscribers, engagement rates, and demographics.

13.5 Approaching Brands and Negotiating Deals

Once you have identified potential brand partners, reach out to them with a personalized and compelling pitch. Clearly articulate how your channel aligns with their brand values and the value you can provide to their marketing goals. Negotiate terms such as deliverables, compensation, exclusivity, and disclosure requirements to ensure a mutually beneficial partnership.

13.6 Crafting Engaging Sponsored Content

When creating sponsored content, it's important to maintain the authenticity and quality that your audience expects. Integrate the brand's messaging seamlessly into your content, ensuring that it feels natural and provides value to your viewers. Use storytelling techniques, demonstrations, or testimonials to showcase the brand's products or services in an engaging and informative way.

13.7 Disclosure and Transparency

Transparency is key when it comes to sponsored content. Comply with the regulations set by your country's advertising standards and disclose your sponsorship clearly and prominently. Use phrases such as "This video is sponsored by..." or "Thanks to our sponsor..." to ensure transparency and maintain trust with your audience.

13.8 Evaluating Brand Fit and Reputation

Before entering into a brand deal, research the brand's reputation, values, and track record. Ensure that the brand aligns with your channel's values and has a positive reputation among consumers. Carefully evaluate whether the brand's products or services genuinely benefit your audience and fit organically within your content.

13.9 Long-Term Partnerships

Building long-term partnerships with brands can be mutually beneficial and provide stability for your channel. Look for opportunities to establish ongoing relationships with brands that align with your content and demonstrate a commitment to supporting your channel's growth. These long-term partnerships can foster trust, creativity, and consistent revenue streams.

13.10 Delivering Value Beyond Sponsorship

Go beyond the scope of a sponsored collaboration by providing additional value to your brand partners. Offer innovative ideas, access to your audience for market research, or suggestions for future product development. By going the extra mile, you can build stronger relationships and establish yourself as a valuable partner.

13.11 Tracking Performance and Results

Measure the success of your sponsored content by tracking performance and results. Use analytics tools to monitor key metrics such as views, engagement rates, click-through rates, and conversions. Evaluate the impact of the sponsored content on your audience, brand sentiment, and overall channel growth. This data will not only help you demonstrate the value of your collaborations to brands but also guide you in refining your future sponsored content strategies.

13.12 Maintaining Authenticity and Audience Trust

Authenticity is paramount when it comes to sponsored content. Your audience trusts you to provide honest and unbiased recommendations. Stay true to your channel's voice and values, and only collaborate with brands and products that genuinely align with your content and resonate with your audience. Continuously communicate with your viewers, address any concerns, and be transparent about your sponsored partnerships to maintain their trust.

13.13 Legal Considerations and Disclosures

Stay informed about the legal obligations and regulations surrounding sponsored content in your country. Familiarize yourself with disclosure requirements and ensure compliance with advertising standards. Clearly disclose your sponsorship in your videos, descriptions, or accompanying social media posts to maintain transparency and adhere to legal obligations.

13.14 Managing Expectations and Relationships

Effectively managing expectations and relationships with brands is essential for long-term success. Clearly communicate your deliverables, timelines, and any specific requirements upfront. Maintain open lines of communication throughout the collaboration, providing updates and seeking feedback. Nurture relationships by delivering on your commitments and going above and beyond to exceed expectations.

13.15 Diversifying Revenue Streams

While sponsored content can be a significant source of revenue, it's essential to diversify your income streams. Explore additional monetization avenues such as merchandise sales, affiliate marketing, fan subscriptions, or crowdfunding. By diversifying your revenue streams, you reduce dependence on brand deals and create a more sustainable income model.

In this chapter, we explored the world of sponsored content and brand deals, emphasizing the importance of maintaining authenticity, transparency, and audience trust. By carefully selecting brand partners, crafting engaging content, and delivering value beyond sponsorships, you can create mutually beneficial collaborations and generate revenue while keeping your audience engaged. In the next chapter, we will delve into the topic of YouTube analytics and how to leverage data to optimize your channel's performance. Stay tuned for Chapter 14: Harnessing the Power of YouTube Analytics.

CHAPTER 14: BUILDING YOUR EMAIL LIST AND MARKETING FUNNEL

Building an email list and creating an effective marketing funnel are essential components of monetizing your YouTube channel and cultivating a dedicated audience. In this chapter, we will explore strategies for capturing email addresses, nurturing relationships with your subscribers, and leveraging your email list to drive engagement and revenue.

14.1 The Importance of an Email List

An email list provides a direct and personalized channel of communication with your audience. Unlike social media platforms, where algorithm changes and platform policies can impact reach, an email list gives you more control over your message and enables you to establish a deeper connection with your subscribers. It serves as a valuable asset for promoting your content, products, and services.

14.2 Creating Opt-In Incentives

To encourage viewers to join your email list, offer valuable opt-in incentives such as exclusive content, downloadable resources, access to a private community, or special discounts. Tailor your incentives to align with your channel's niche and the interests of your target audience. Emphasize the unique value they will receive by subscribing to your email list.

14.3 Placing Opt-In Forms Strategically

Strategically place opt-in forms on your YouTube channel, website, and other online platforms to maximize visibility and conversions. Consider embedding sign-up forms within video descriptions, dedicated landing pages, sidebar widgets, or pop-up overlays. Experiment with different placements and monitor their effectiveness using analytics tools.

14.4 Crafting Compelling Email Content

Once you have captured email addresses, focus on delivering valuable and engaging content to your subscribers. Craft personalized and well-designed emails that resonate with your audience. Provide updates on your latest videos, behind-the-scenes insights, exclusive content, and promotions. Keep your emails concise, visually appealing, and easy to navigate.

14.5 Nurturing Subscriber Relationships

Building strong relationships with your subscribers is crucial for long-term success. Regularly engage with your email list by sending consistent and relevant content. Encourage two-way communication by inviting feedback, responding to emails, and addressing subscriber questions. Make your subscribers feel valued and appreciated for being part of your community.

14.6 Segmentation and Personalization

Segmenting your email list based on subscriber interests, demographics, or engagement levels allows for more targeted and personalized communication. Customize your email content and offers to cater to different segments, ensuring that each subscriber receives content that is most relevant and valuable to them. This approach increases open rates, click-through rates, and overall engagement.

14.7 Email Automation and Sequences

Utilize email automation and sequences to streamline your communication and deliver timely messages. Set up automated welcome emails for new subscribers, drip campaigns to nurture leads, or triggered emails based on specific actions or milestones. Automation saves time and ensures consistent and timely communication with your audience.

14.8 Promoting Products and Services

Your email list can be a powerful tool for promoting your products, services, or affiliate offerings. However, strike a balance between providing value and promoting your offerings. Focus on educating and solving problems for your subscribers, and weave your product or service promotions naturally into your email content. Provide exclusive discounts or bonuses to incentivize purchases.

14.9 Analyzing Email Performance

Regularly analyze key metrics such as open rates, click-through rates, conversion rates, and unsubscribe rates to assess the effectiveness of your email campaigns. Use A/B testing to experiment with different subject lines, content formats, or call-to-action buttons. Gather insights from analytics tools and subscriber feedback to refine your email marketing strategy.

14.10 Integrating Social Media and YouTube

Leverage your email list to drive engagement and growth on your social media platforms and YouTube channel. Include social media buttons and YouTube subscribe links in your emails to encourage subscribers to connect with you on other platforms. Cross-promote your content and encourage your subscribers to share your videos or follow you on social media. This integrated approach helps you expand your reach, strengthen your brand presence, and foster a sense of community across multiple platforms.

14.11 Monetizing Your Email List

Beyond promoting your own products and services, consider monetizing your email list through affiliate marketing or sponsored email campaigns. Partner with relevant brands or businesses that align with your audience's interests and values. Carefully select partnerships that provide genuine value to your subscribers and maintain the trust you have established.

14.12 GDPR Compliance and Data Privacy

Ensure that your email marketing practices comply with applicable data privacy regulations, such as the General Data Protection Regulation (GDPR) for European subscribers. Obtain proper consent for collecting and using personal data, provide clear privacy policies, and offer opt-out options. Prioritize data security and implement measures to protect the information you gather.

14.13 Growing and Scaling Your Email List

Continuously focus on growing and scaling your email list to expand your reach and increase your revenue potential. Employ various strategies such as optimizing your website for conversions, running targeted advertising campaigns, collaborating with other creators for cross-promotion, or hosting contests or giveaways to encourage sign-ups. Regularly assess and refine your tactics based on data and feedback.

14.14 Building a Marketing Funnel

A marketing funnel is a step-by-step process that guides your audience from awareness to conversion. Develop a well-structured marketing funnel that aligns with your content and monetization goals. Map out the stages, such as awareness, consideration, and decision, and create content and email sequences tailored to each stage to nurture leads and drive conversions.

14.15 Testing, Iterating, and Optimizing

Effective email marketing requires ongoing testing, iterating, and optimization. Experiment with different strategies, content formats, subject lines, and CTAs to identify what resonates best with your audience. Regularly review your email performance, analyze user behavior, and seek feedback from your subscribers to make data-driven decisions and continually improve your email marketing efforts.

In this chapter, we explored the significance of building an email list and creating a robust marketing funnel to monetize your YouTube channel. By capturing email addresses, nurturing relationships with your subscribers, and leveraging targeted email campaigns, you can cultivate a loyal audience, drive engagement, and generate revenue. In the next chapter, we will delve into the knowledge of scaling your channel beyond youtube.

CHAPTER 15: SCALING YOUR CHANNEL: BEYOND YOUTUBE

While YouTube serves as a powerful platform for content creators, scaling your channel goes beyond just YouTube itself. In this final chapter, we will explore strategies to expand your presence and diversify your revenue streams beyond the YouTube platform.

15.1 Establishing a Website or Blog

Creating a dedicated website or blog allows you to showcase your content, provide additional resources, and connect with your audience on a more personal level. It serves as a hub where you can share in-depth articles, behind-the-scenes stories, merchandise offerings, and links to your YouTube videos. A website or blog also improves your discoverability on search engines, driving organic traffic to your channel.

15.2 Engaging with Social Media Platforms

Expand your reach and engagement by leveraging social media platforms to complement your YouTube presence. Choose platforms that align with your content and target audience, such as Instagram, Twitter, Facebook, or TikTok. Develop a social media strategy to share snippets of your videos, behind-the-scenes content, teasers, and engage with your audience in real-time. Cross-promote your YouTube channel on social media and encourage followers to subscribe.

15.3 Exploring Podcasting

Podcasting is a rapidly growing medium that allows you to reach a new audience and provide content in an audio format. Consider repurposing your YouTube content into podcast episodes or creating exclusive podcast episodes to complement your channel. Podcasting provides an opportunity to delve deeper into topics, interview experts, and connect with your audience in a more intimate and portable way.

15.4 Writing a Book or E-book

If you have valuable expertise or a compelling story to share, consider writing a book or e-book. This not only establishes you as an authority in your niche but also creates an additional revenue stream. Your YouTube channel can serve as a platform to promote and market your book, driving sales and expanding your audience beyond the confines of video content.

15.5 Hosting Workshops or Online Courses

Leverage your expertise and the trust you have built with your audience by hosting workshops or creating online courses. Develop educational content that provides value and helps your audience achieve specific goals. These workshops or courses can be monetized through enrollment fees or subscriptions, offering your audience an opportunity to dive deeper into the subjects you cover on your YouTube channel.

15.6 Speaking Engagements and Events

As your channel grows, you may receive opportunities to speak at conferences, industry events, or even host your own live events. Embrace these opportunities to connect with your audience face-to-face, expand your network, and further establish your authority in your niche. Speaking engagements and events provide a platform to share your knowledge, inspire others, and create memorable experiences for your community.

15.7 Licensing and Merchandising

Consider licensing your content or creating merchandise to capitalize on your brand's popularity. Explore partnerships with companies interested in using your content for commercial purposes, such as featuring your videos in advertisements or licensing your brand for products. Additionally, develop a line of branded merchandise, including clothing, accessories, or digital products, to offer your audience a tangible way to support your channel while promoting your brand.

15.8 Collaborations and Partnerships

Collaborating with other creators, brands, or organizations can significantly expand your reach and introduce you to new audiences. Seek collaborations that align with your values and target audience, and create mutually beneficial partnerships that leverage each other's strengths. Collaborations can include co-creating content, cross-promoting each other's channels, or even embarking on joint projects or campaigns.

15.9 Managing Your Brand and Business

As you scale your channel and diversify your revenue streams, it becomes increasingly important to manage your brand and business effectively. Consider establishing a formal business entity, consult with professionals such as lawyers or accountants, and implement proper systems for financial management, content scheduling, and audience analytics. Treat your channel as a business and prioritize strategic planning, goal setting, and regular evaluation of your performance. Stay informed about industry trends, algorithm changes, and emerging platforms to adapt and stay ahead in the ever-evolving digital landscape.

15.10 Hiring a Team or Outsourcing

As your channel grows and your workload increases, you may find it beneficial to hire a team or outsource certain tasks. Consider hiring editors, graphic designers, social media managers, or virtual assistants to help streamline your content creation process, enhance your branding, and manage administrative tasks. Delegating responsibilities allows you to focus on creating high-quality content and expanding your channel's reach.

15.11 Continuing Education and Personal Growth

To stay relevant and continuously improve as a content creator, invest in your own personal growth and education. Attend workshops, conferences, or online courses related to content creation, digital marketing, or your niche. Stay curious, seek feedback from your audience, and embrace a mindset of lifelong learning. Constantly honing your skills and staying ahead of industry trends will contribute to your long-term success.

15.12 Evaluating and Adapting

Regularly evaluate the performance of your channel, revenue streams, and expansion efforts. Analyze audience engagement, revenue sources, and the effectiveness of different strategies. Use data-driven insights to identify what is working well and what needs improvement. Adapt your approach, pivot when necessary, and be open to trying new ideas to optimize your channel's growth and profitability.

15.13 Balancing Quality and Quantity

As you explore various avenues for scaling your channel, it's crucial to strike a balance between quality and quantity. While consistent content creation is important for maintaining engagement, ensure that you don't compromise on the quality of your videos or other offerings. Focus on providing value to your audience, delivering content that resonates, and maintaining the authenticity and integrity of your brand.

15.14 Embracing a Long-Term Mindset

Scaling your channel and diversifying your revenue streams is a long-term endeavor. Embrace patience, persistence, and a long-term mindset. Success rarely happens overnight, and building a sustainable and profitable channel takes time, effort, and dedication. Stay committed to your vision, adapt to changes along the way, and celebrate milestones and achievements on your journey.

In this final chapter, we explored strategies for scaling your channel beyond YouTube itself. By establishing a website, leveraging social media platforms, exploring podcasting, creating additional revenue streams, and managing your brand and business effectively, you can expand your presence, reach new audiences, and generate diversified income. Remember, the path to success is unique for every content creator, so embrace experimentation, stay true to your voice, and continue to provide value to your audience. Best of luck on your journey to scaling your channel and achieving your goals!

www.ingramcontent.com/pod-product-compliance
Lightning Source LLC
Chambersburg PA
CBHW031542210526
45464CB00003B/1109